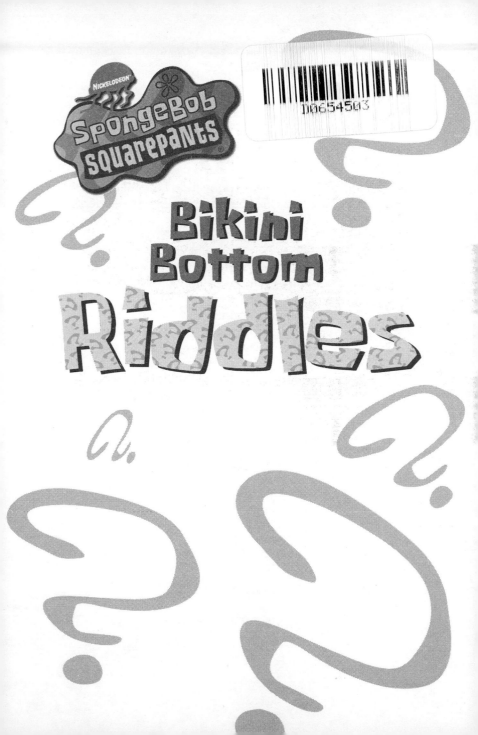

NICKELODEON

SpongeBob SquarePants

Bikini Bottom Riddles

00654593

Based on the TV series SpongeBob SquarePants
created by Stephen Hillenburg as seen on Nickelodeon

SIMON AND SCHUSTER
First published in Great Britain in 2006
by Simon & Schuster UK Ltd
Africa House, 64-78 Kingsway, London WC2B 6AH

Originally published in the USA in 2005 by
Simon Spotlight, an imprint of Simon & Schuster
Children's Division, New York.

A CIP catalogue record for this book is
available from the British Library

ISBN 1 41691679 2
EAN 9781416916796

Printed by Cox & Wyman Ltd, Reading, Berks

1 3 5 7 9 10 8 6 4 2

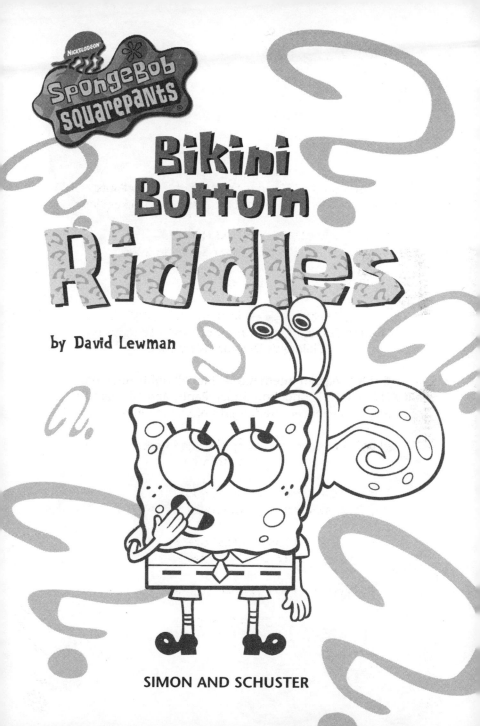

SpongeBob SquarePants

Bikini Bottom Riddles

by David Lewman

SIMON AND SCHUSTER

Why doesn't SpongeBob have to pay his electric bill?

Because his pineapple house never runs out of juice!

Sandy: Knock-knock.

Patrick: Who's there?

Sandy: Funnel.

Patrick: Funnel who?

Sandy: Fun'll break out the minute SpongeBob gets here!

4

Why is Sandy Friends with SpongeBob and Patrick?
Because squirrels love nuts!

Why does SpongeBob love mushrooms?
Because there's FUN in every FUNgus!

5

Why does SpongeBob
keep toys in the
refrigerator?
So he can play it cool.

Why did Plankton
push a toy toward
Patrick with a stick?
He was trying to poke
fun at him.

Patrick: Knock-knock.

Sandy: Who's there?

Patrick: Plane.

Sandy: Plane who?

Patrick: Playin' with SpongeBob is my favourite thing to do!

Why did SpongeBob set up his games outside a haunted house?
He wanted to play by the ghouls.

Patrick: Knock-knock.
SpongeBob: Who's there?
Patrick: Ice.
SpongeBob: Ice who?
Patrick: Ice cream, please!

Why do SpongeBob and Patrick like to eat together?
So they can be taste buds.

Patrick: Knock-knock.

SpongeBob: Who's there?

Patrick: Pile.

SpongeBob: Pile who?

Patrick: Pie'll go great with this ice cream!

Why does Patrick always fall asleep when SpongeBob beats him in a game?
He's a snore loser.

Patrick: Knock-knock.

SpongeBob: Who's there?

Patrick: Sir.

SpongeBob: Sir who?

Patrick: Surprise! It's me!

Why did Patrick build a house out of cheese?
So he'd have cottage cheese.

If Patrick were an outlaw, who would he be?
Belly the Kid.

What is Patrick's breakfast specialty?
Belchin' waffles.

Who invented the gas-powered telephone?
Alexander Graham Belch.

What did Patrick win at the belching contest?
A burp certificate.

Why did Patrick climb up the side of the Fish?
He wanted to be king of the gill.

Why are mornings tough in Patrick's house?
You always get off to a rocky start.

What kind of stone is the best to sleep on?
Bedrock.

Why did Patrick move out from under the green stone?
It turned out to be a sham rock.

What do you get when you cross Squidward with a wasp?
A grumble bee.

If Squidward were a plant, what kind would he be?
A grumble weed.

What group did Squidward join when he was young?
The Snub Scouts.

Squidward: Knock-knock.

Mr Krabs: Who's there?

Squidward: Snob.

Mr Krabs: Snob who?

Squidward: This knob's so greasy I can't open the door.

What crime did the police arrest Squidward for?

Six armed snobberies.

Why did SpongeBob strap a watch to his shoe? So he was always on time.

Squidward: Knock-knock.
SpongeBob: Who's there?
Squidward: Walleye.
SpongeBob: Walleye who?
Squidward: While I nap, you work.

What does Squidward use to turn his boat?
The sneering wheel.

Why did SpongeBob have to stop driving at the end of the day?
He ran out of class.

How does Mrs
Puff feel when
she gives
exams?
Testy.

Why did Mrs Puff feel
crazy after SpongeBob's
license test?
He drove her up a wall.

Why can't Mrs Puff understand SpongeBob?
Because she never knows what he's driving at.

What do you call someone with a boating license in Bikini Bottom?
A deep-sea driver.

What does Mr. Krabs love to drive?
A hard bargain.

How is Plankton like
Squidward's ink?
They're both little squirts.

Why won't Plankton ever make a big splash?
Because he's a little drip.

What does Plankton chew between meals?
Bubble chum.

21

Why did the Fish stop eating worms?
He was trying to lose bait.

Why are Fish always making excuses?
To get off the hook.

What do you call baby Fish in sauce?
Tartar tots.

Which fish is the cheapest?
The stingy ray.

Which kind of seal is the most musical?
The harp seal.

What did the seal princess lose at the ball?
Her glass flipper.

What do fish ride at the playground?
The teeter-tartar.

Which fish is the heaviest?
The goldfish.

Which fish is the most fetching?
The dogfish.

What did the witch do to the Fish?
She cast a smell on him.

What did SpongeBob get when he tried using karate on a pig?
A pork chop.

How did the hammerhead shark do on his exam?
He nailed it.

Which vegetable is the funniest?
The artijoke.

Why did the tomato fall on Patrick?
It wanted to squish upon a star.

What did SpongeBob say
when he found the kitchen
floor covered in tomatoes?
"There's something squishy
going on here."

What's brown and delicious and really dangerous?
A chocolate milk shark.

Which kind of salt should never be used during meals?
The somersault.

How did the salt Feel when it met the French Fries?
Shaken.

Why was
SpongeBob
afraid of the
Krabby Patty
buns?

They looked seedy.

How do you get answers
out of a Krabby Patty?

You grill it.

What is SpongeBob's
Favourite bedtime story?
Hansel and Griddle.

Why did SpongeBob
add bubble soap to his
pancakes?
He wanted to blow his stack.

How did the Krabby
Patty feel by the end
of the workday?
Totally fried.

How did Squidward
feel about the world's
tiniest pickle?
It was no big dill.

Which sea can give you gas?
The CaribBEAN.

Which ocean can make you laugh?
The Atlantickle.

Which ocean is the most detailed?
The Specific Ocean.

Why did the whale drink hot water?
She wanted to blow off steam.

Which Fish is best at answering doors?
The halibutler.

Which Fish is the best at boxing?
The sockeye salmon.

Which Fish has the shortest temper?
The snapper.

Which fish does the best imitations?
The parrot fish.

Which fish is the clumsiest?
The Flounder.

Which fish makes the best shoes?
The sole.

What's it called when you trip in Bikini Bottom?

A waterfall.

What's the best kind of water to sleep on?
Spring water.

What's the best kind of water to dance on?
Tap water.

Sandy: Did you hear about the robber with the messy hair?

SpongeBob: Yeah, he was thrown in gel.

Patrick: What did the key say to the door?

Mr Krabs: "Things are locking up."

SpongeBob: Knock-knock.

Sandy: Who's there?

SpongeBob: Beach.

Sandy: Beach who?

SpongeBob: Beach you to the Goo Lagoon!

Why doesn't Bubble Buddy like to bake?
He's afraid of rolling pins.

Which musical notes does Bubble Buddy like least?
The sharps.

What kind of candy should you never give to Bubble Buddy?

A lollipop.

Why is Squidward like a
lollipop on the ceiling?
He's stuck-up.

What do sea snakes do
after a fight?
They hiss and make up.

Which snake makes
the best dessert?
The pie-thon.

Why did Patchy the Pirate jiggle the treasure chest?
He wanted to shake his booty.

What says "ahr," steals treasure, and tastes delicious?
A cherry pirate.

What is Patchy the Pirate's best basketball move?

His hook shot.

Why did SpongeBob go
to JellyFish Fields?
To hear the latest buzz.

SpongeBob: Knock-knock.

Patrick: Who's there?

SpongeBob: Sam.

Patrick: Sam who?

SpongeBob: Salmon are coming this way—let's leave.

THE END